This book is written for those who have dreams of being rich. You simply *cannot* do it by working for someone else—you have to be in business for yourself. But how do you do it?

You have a family so you can't go back to school; you have little or no money so you can't make a loan to start a business; you can make better than a good living in sales, but you're not a salesman. The answer is Network Marketing.

This book is a *no-nonsense account* of the good and the bad about Network Marketing. It tells you the truth—how you can make it, how you can fail, why you might have failed in the past and how to do it the right way *this* time.

I'd rather face *five bikers in a back alley* than use the *old* methods of Network Marketing. So, I'll give you the *new* methods that, *coupled with the old*, can't miss.

I'll tell you the basics, why it's the best it has *ever* been and how YOU can become rich. Of course, I can't guarantee that because, it's up to you. But . . .

Anyone Can Do It!

Author: Pete Billac
Editors: Ken Harris, Bill Jones
Layout Artist: Kimberly Morrison, Sharon Davis
Cover Design: John Gilmore

OTHER BOOKS BY PETE BILLAC:

The Annihilator
The Last Medal of Honor
How Not to be Lonely—TONIGHT
All About Cruises
New Father's Baby Guide
Willie the Wisp
Lose Fat While You Sleep
Managing Stress
Y2K: A World in Crisis? (Published)

Copyright @ August 1999
Swan Publishing
Library of Congress Catalog Card #99-65295
ISBN# 0-943629-41-1

THE NEW MILLIONAIRES is available in quantity discounts through Swan Publishing, 126 Live Oak, Alvin, TX 77511. Phone: (281) 388-2547, Fax: (281) 585-3738, or e-mail : swanbooks@ghg.net. URL: http://www.swan-pub.com

Printed in the United States of America.

DEDICATION

To EVERYONE involved in Network Marketing; you make things happen. You WANT to be successful and I like being around you.

The belief you have in yourself and your chosen company is commendable and I wish you success (or continued success). I hope to meet all of you someday.

I dedicate this book to you. You are alive and free and fun and enthusiastic about everything you do. You are very special human beings.

In most books, this is a blank page. I wanted to use it to explain my *style* of writing. I write with words that are CAPITALIZED, *italicized*, **bold faced** and with "quotation marks." Since most of my books are in the *How-To* category, I want to make ABSOLUTELY certain that there is **no room** for even a *hint* of MISIN-TERPRETATION. Let me explain why.

As a kid in grade school, teachers said I had a fantastic memory; not smart, you understand—a good MEMORY. I *remember* a six-line example of how a single word—EMPHASIZED—changes the meaning of the entire sentence: I NEVER SAID HE STOLE THAT!

I never said he stole that!
I **NEVER** said he stole that!
I never **SAID** he stole that!
I never said **HE** stole that!
I never said he **STOLE** that!
I never said he stole **THAT**!

And THAT, my critics, professional writers, and English teachers is **why** I chose to put the *emphasis* on certain words. Just blame it on *my* "writing style."

FOREWORD

This book will tell you the truth in plain words. It tells the good and the bad about Network Marketing. By "telling it the way it is" you can decide for yourself whether this industry is for you or not.

If you are already IN Network Marketing, I think I can help you become successful—or **more** successful. No matter how much money you are presently making, I'll tell you the *smartest* and *easiest* methods to make more.

And to those who are just "thinking" of getting into Network Marketing, I will answer your questions truthfully and candidly and teach you to the ways to do it CORRECTLY. In short, I give you the best CHANCE at being successful. I can't *guarantee* your success, only YOU can do that.

On the first page as you opened this book, I made the comment that "I'd rather fight five bikers in a back alley than work this business the way *most* have worked it in the past—the *hard* way." That's a fact that might be a bit overstated, but you understand what I'm trying to say.

My methods, the NEW way *coupled* with the OLD, is breathtaking; it's *easier*, it's *smarter* and it's *quicker*. Most of all, it takes the SELLING out of a sales organization and allows you only to TELL. Thus, non-salespersons can make a fortune also.

I'll share with you some secrets that not only make Network Marketing EASIER, but more profitable and much more FUN! You just have to read, understand, and BELIEVE!

I like people. I like it even *more* if people like me.

I would *never* get in a business where I have to bother, badger, pursue, persuade, cajole, coerce, trick, beg, threaten or LIE to people to SELL them anything.

MY way or succeeding in Network Marketing is both old *and* new—and both work! Yes, separately, they each work well, but *together,* they can't miss—IF you prepare yourself to become rich and IF you follow some of the basics.

Of course, there's work involved and oftentimes *hard* work; nobody who knows says it's easy. It's not easy to become a millionaire; if it was, EVERYBODY would be rich!

My dad once told me that *work, works.* He was wrong. My high school math teacher told me that *hard work, works.* He, too, wasn't *exactly* right. But my football coach had the answer; he said *smart work, works.* Well, I've found that *hard, smart work* can't miss! The trick is, to enjoy yourself while earning a lot of money.

How would you like to get rich with a small investment? With NO boss? NO college degree? NO sales ability? NO driving to and from work each day? NO childcare services to pay?

For a single parent, how nice it is to be at home with your small children. Or AT home to greet your kids when they return from school. Being HOME is important for children during their formative years, but in these inflationary times it's often necessary that both parents work to survive.

Wouldn't it be nice if mom was at home? Wouldn't it be NICER if mom AND dad were at home? If you absolutely can't be home, why not try a *part-time* job that could make you as much as you are making full-time? These are but some of the great advantages of a home-based business.

How about being able to TAKE OFF from work whenever *you* want, and to work as hard as *you'd* like knowing that the more you work the more money you make? No need to buy new clothes, dress up—even *get* dressed—if you choose not to. These are but *some* of the advantages of having your own business where you work out of your house.

The biggest advantage of working for yourself is that you can—with smart, hard work, a plan, a system, and right direction—get rich, and make enough to guarantee a nice retirement for yourself and a comfortable life for those you love.

All of this is truly possible in Network Marketing. Read this book from cover to cover, then go back to the parts that are important to you. I tell it all. Just follow my system and you'll make it happen.

And know at the onset that I do NOT represent any Network Marketing company nor do I sell any products. This book is meant to help the entire industry, and it will help YOU become a NEW MILLIONAIRE IF you follow the system and work smart and hard.

Please don't hesitate for a chance to change your life and lifestyle for the better. There are some excellent opportunities "out there" and this book tells how to recognize them.

To be rich—to become a millionaire in ANY business—requires, effort, time, smart thinking, planning, correct decisions, and perseverance. Good luck and God bless you.

Pete Billac

TABLE OF CONTENTS

Chapter 1
ANYONE CAN DO IT

THE BASICS

I think the easiest way to explain Network Marketing is people talking with people, who talk with people, who talk with people, who talk with more people, etc. It's a whole line of people **telling** people about the product(s) or services they represent.

To begin, it's a *home-based business;* you are working for yourself. This means you don't need a store, newspaper or televison ads or employees. It isn't necessary to drive to and from work, wear special clothes, or even *bathe* if you don't want to. Some of the most successful network marketers I've met never leave their homes. They DUPLICATE their system and themselves.

I learned how this duplication method worked when I read (somewhere) about a person who was hired to dig postholes for a large fence company. He was paid $10 a hole. No matter how hard or how fast he worked, it seems that 10 holes per day was his maximum. The most he could ever expect to earn was $100 a day. And, the company needed more holes dug for more fenceposts to remain in business.

So, this enterprising young man found five of his friends who needed a job and he hired them to dig holes for **$9** each. He showed them how to do it; he

DUPLICATED himself. He still earned his $100 a day digging his own holes, but also $10 from each of his five employees or $50 a day extra from them. They did the same as he.

They each found five people (25 total) who were digging 10 holes a day for $8 a hole. NOW, he earned his same $100 from his efforts, plus he was taking in $50 from his five workers, and he was NOW getting **another** $1 a hole times 10 holes from 25 workers or TWO HUNDRED AND FIFTY DOLLARS per day from *their* efforts.

To take it one step further, each of THOSE 25, hired five people each (jobs weren't plentiful then) to dig the same holes for $7 a day. Want to figure that out? I'll do it for you. He had 125 more hole-diggers earning him an additional $1 per hole times 10 holes or TWELVE HUNDRED AND FIFTY DOLLARS PER DAY!

That little beginning hole-digger with NO money, just DUPLICATION, needn't dig any more holes. His job then was to watch over the diggers, cheer them on, and replace the ones who quit. He was taking in more than FIFTEEN HUNDRED DOLLARS a day! He began working *hard* and graduated to working *smart*. Here's another, almost unbelievable example of duplication.

Whether you play golf or not is unimportant; just know that there are 18 holes on a regulation course. Let's say someone talks to you about making a wager on a game. You agree to start with betting a PENNY on the first hole, doubling the bet all the way through.

Seems safe enough, right?

The LAST HOLE plays for over
THIRTEEN HUNDRED DOLLARS!

Don't believe it? Check it with your calculator. That, my friends, is the power of DUPLICATION and Network Marketing. That is how YOU can become rich if you work hard *and* smart. That's what I'm going to share with you in this book. Read and learn. It could make you wealthy, or at the very least, change your lifestyle to where you never have to read that menu *from right to left* ever again.

If you're the cautious type, work at it part time. Then, when you start earning *three times* more than you are making at your present job—for more than six months—and you enjoy being in business for yourself, *quit* that regular job and do this full time.

HOW IT ALL BEGINS

Usually, it's when you are first *dragged* by a friend or relative to one of these "opportunity" meetings and there is some silver-tongued devil telling how you can earn $10,000 up to $50,000 a month (or more) in *this* company if you follow directions and work at it.

"This is a bunch of bull," you say. Perhaps. But I've seen it happen over and over and OVER again by the most unlikely people one could imagine could ever earn more than minimum wage.

Yes, this DOES happen—often. And, for every person earning this kind of money after just 12 to 18 months, there are tens of thousands making $3,000 to $5,000 a month and many more earning $1,000 or $2,000 a month. Some, of course, are *losing* money or making only expenses.

More people LOSE money than make money in *most* home-based business that first year; in fact, it's the same in *most* first-time businesses because they make any of a series of errors.

It's no different in Network Marketing other than the ones who fail have someone *else* to blame other than themselves.

If you are SINCERE about making money, I wholeheartedly recommend that you TRY Network Marketing. Just read this book with an open mind and forget what you've heard from others, or a failure or two you experienced in the past, because *that was then and this is now!*

Everything has changed and it is getting better as we breathe. If you *did* try and fail, perhaps you're not right for Network Marketing, or what you did was make some very *unwise* decisions.

PAST MISTAKES

Lets's begin with those who were in Network Marketing two or three times (or more) and failed at it.

Just to start with a clean slate, let's try to determine which of the following errors you were guilty of:

- ❖ **Became involved with the wrong company**
- ❖ **The wrong product**
- ❖ **You didn't work hard or smart**
- ❖ **You had no direction or training**
- ❖ **You didn't take time to learn and work the *system***

I know there could be other (personal) reasons for your failure other than these, but these are sufficient for you to get the idea.

This book teaches you how to choose the RIGHT company, the RIGHT product, *and* how to really EARN money. Additionally, you will know *exactly* what to expect from your efforts!

HOW MUCH YOU CAN EARN

This, of course, is impossible to tell because we're all different. How much time and study and effort are you prepared to put into it? I can, however, give you a few examples of what others have done and then, it's up to you.

Almost anyone can make big money in Network Marketing. I know hundreds of people, *personally,* who are making a quarter of a million dollars a year in less than **two years** with a Network Marketing company. Match THAT with a college degree—in almost anything?

And remember, I'm not trying *sell* you anything

or interest you into joining my company; I have no company! My *business* is selling books and you already bought this one; I'm just trying to give you the secrets of making big money in an industry that is changing the way people buy things.

Now, think who *you* know who is earning $250,000 a year or more—*legally*—without a college degree, marrying into it, playing sports, being in the movies, winning the lotto or who began their business with less than $500 and who hasn't been working most of their life at the same business.

I have a friend who was a PIZZA DELIVERY BOY two years ago and he is now earning about $30,000—*a month!* I know a *blind lady* who is 83 years old and she is earning about $7,000 a month in her Network Marketing company after one year.

I know a husband and wife team who were both school teachers for over 20 years and their first year in Network Marketing they earned over $600,000. I could go on and on but *phooey* on them, they're making it, let's talk about you and how YOU can do the same or better. Is it REALLY possible! **YES, it is!**

All *you* have to do is be willing to learn, put in the time, and work hard AND smart. Hard work is great and you'll earn *some* money working hard no matter how many mistakes you make. But SMART work is better. And, hard, smart work simply cannot fail IF you have the right vehicle.

THE RIGHT COMPANY

At least three times a week I am called, faxed or e.mailed some new "business opportunity" that will make me rich. I'm already rich—or as rich as I need to be. And, I am NO Network Marketer; I'm a *teacher* of Network Marketing; I'm a coach, not a player. I'm in the book business, the *people* business, and I market my books.

When people call up with such enthusiasm about their new product and/or company, and tell me how terrific it is, I listen. Of *course* it's the best, it's *their* chosen company—and chances are with this enthusi- asm, they'll *make* it work. This doesn't mean, however, that this company is the best for you!

The first thing I need to know is *why* their company is the best. Exactly how much *research* has this excited caller done on the background of the company? On its officers? On the product? How long has it been in business? What is their compensation plan? How many distributors does it have? Better yet, how *much* are these distributors making?

Chances are they know NONE of these an- swers. They attended a meeting and "heard"what the person in the front of the room told them and they liked the product and felt that they could sell it. And their *friend* who brought them to the meeting said it was okay. Actually, that's the FIRST answer they need to find out about—the product.

THE PRODUCT

My research on Network Marketing has been over more than four decades. Without a doubt, the FIRST thing you look for is a company with a *unique* product or service that nobody else has. It could also be something that almost everyone NEEDS (or wants) that is CHEAPER and/or can be delivered faster than a competitive product. To appeal to the majority, that product or service must make them:

☆ **Feel better**
☆ **Look better**
☆ **Live longer**
☆ **Get things done quicker**
☆ **Enjoy life more**
☆ **Increase their gasoline mileage**
☆ **Save them money**

The product is vital. Think about it. If the product is the same as *everyone else is selling*, what are your odds? It's smart to choose a product the MAJORITY wants or needs. Think of any number of PRODUCTS, ones that work, that are safe and legal—that **you** would be inclined to buy.

FINANCIAL BACKING

The company must have MONEY behind it. I do, however, know of several successful companies that began with a few people who pooled their credit cards and built a terrific organization, but for each one that succeeded, tens of thousands did not. Of ALL the companies that started on a shoestring, most ended up *hanging themselves* with that same string. *Research* the company as best you can

There are many unexpected pitfalls in starting a new business and without backup money, if you make any number of mistakes along the way and if you don't have sufficient capital to "weather this storm," you are **out of business!**

COMPENSATION PLAN

On any job, one of the first few answers you need to get is, *How much money do I make? How do I get paid? When?* I will spend much time talking about money, because that's what we're really talking about. How much MONEY can you earn in this business with this company.

Again, everyone thinks *their* plan is best. The fact is, *most* Network Marketers *don't understand their own compensation plan* and couldn't explain it if their life depended upon it. They get involved in a company because a friend *sells* them on the program and too much of the time the friend doesn't understand what they are talking about. People are *naive*. Many are just plain dumb.

They hear someone give a good speech, the person who brought them *to* the meeting (whether they've heard the speech a *thousand* times or more) will sit next to them and smile and laugh at tired jokes they've heard over and over that simply cannot *still* be funny, and they get their friend to sign a paper and join and *then* they discuss the compensation plan.

If you just want to *buy* whatever they are selling and want to get it wholesale, sign and get the stuff and try it. But if you plan on it bringing income, FIND OUT what you're going to make and UNDERSTAND how it works BEFORE you make any blind commitment. That's part of the RESEARCH I suggest you do.

Remember, people lose at ANYTHING they try if they are greedy or stupid. EVERY time I've lost at something, it's been one of these two reasons. I either thought I'd make a "killing" with little effort or investment or, I didn't do my RESEARCH into the product, the compensation plan, the officers or their backup money to overcome their mistakes. And, they WILL make mistakes; every new business does. Here is what I recommend as far as the compensation plan:

Have it explained to you *over and over* until you understand it. If there's doubt, ask the *next* person who tries to interest you in Network Marketing and get *their* opinion on it.

If you are in Network Marketing, *somebody* in the organization you are being courted to join will understand and be able to explain these plans to you. Enlist their help and listen to an explanation until you understand the plan completely. Remember, we're talking about money, and money counts.

LEARNING and TRAINING

No matter how hard or smart you work, the first rule of selling is that you KNOW what you're talking about. If not, how can you possibly tell others? You NEED to learn. Read the literature, listen to tapes, watch videos, attend meetings and training sessions and listen to what the one who sponsored you tells you. If you discover that they don't know what they're talking about or they neglect you, go to the one who sponsored *them*. You NEED proper training!

INTEGRITY and ABILITY

The next "ingredient" is the INTEGRITY and ABILITY of the company's corporate officers. Without *qualified, experienced* officers with INTEGRITY, a company rarely becomes successful. You NEED corporate officers who KNOW what they're doing, who care about YOU, who work hard and who are good people. Where can you find all of this? It's out there. You just have to look BEFORE you make a choice.

GREEDY or STUPID

Please don't fault me for my candor; this book is meant to help you, not insult you. What you can always expect from me is the truth and oftentimes there is not a delicate way to tell the truth.

I know I said this before but it needs saying again. *The only times I've lost on an investment was when I was either greedy or stupid—or both. I either thought I could "make a killing" with little effort or didn't do my homework. When I am going to invest time and money in anything, the first thing I do is RESEARCH.*

I would have to believe that the individual introducing me to this new Network Marketing company was an intelligent person with integrity. Also, I would have to like and want to use the product and see if I could afford (or want to take) the time required to become involved. Then, I'd set goals (surmountable ones). Remember, deal with this new venture as if it is—a business.

There's a saying, *"If you don't TAKE a chance, you never HAVE a chance!"* That one might not always apply in business UNLESS you have the time and money to lose and you shoot for the stars. If you take that chance without research, it's a coin toss.

So, don't be sour on Network Marketing if it didn't work for you previously. It is still the *best chance* a "regular" person has to be financially independent, with very little money invested and virtually no previous experience or skills.

Chapter 2
BEWARE

NON-BELIEVERS

You will always run into people who just *do not believe* that Network Marketing works. Don't be offended by them, understand them and pray for them. *They just don't know that they don't know*!

Most are conservatives, or naive wage-earners who have no earthly conception of HOW Network Marketing works. They could never, not in their wildest dreams, reason that *anyone* other than movie stars, CEO's of giant corporations, star athletes, or dope dealers could make 10, or 15, or 20 THOUSAND dollars a month! These folks you can *never* convince. Don't try!

Can you imagine my telling them that I run into Network Marketers each WEEK who are earning $30,000 a MONTH during bad years? Thousands of them are driving luxury cars, living in mansions, and going on vacations for a *full month* only to return and find that they have more money in the bank than they had before they left!

Think they'd believe that one my friends was "stuck at" about $3000 a month after 17 months and within five months of using my new easy methods couple with the age-old system, his check jumped to

$36,000—a MONTH! The leaders in these many companies who worked smart and hard—who put in the hours and the time—are earning well over a MILLION dollars a year? If you told these non-believers that, they would swear that think you were lying, crazy or stupid. But, it's true.

These non-believers are, mostly, the ones who never take a chance. They graduated from college, got a job, and that's all they know. They are either satisfied with their present job or won't tell you if they're not. Don't make fun of them, they're EVERYWHERE. No amount of convincing will alter their thinking, just pass them up. To prove that they REALLY don't know, they tell you that you are working a PYRAMID SCHEME.

PYRAMIDS

Before we get too far into this book, let's put something to rest—PERMANENTLY! Network Marketing **IS NOT** A PYRAMID SCHEME!

I can always spot a person who knows ABSO-LUTELY NOTHING about this industry when they talk about a *pyramid,* but, bless their hearts, they *heard* of people losing in a pyramid scheme and they confuse it with Network Marketing.

First of all, the so-called "pyramid scheme" is ILLEGAL! The very first thing an attorney general in any state looks for before the paint with his name on the door dries, is a company where people sell people something that involves putting up money and no product is involved. The only ones who make money with these *schemes* are the ones at the top. Everyone else just contributes!

Egyptians built the true pyramids; they started at the bottom and built UP. With Network Marketing, you build like the Egyptians; start at the bottom and work up. And, *yes*, Network Marketing IS work. I never even implied that it was *easy* work, I only promised you the OPPORTUNITY to make a lot of money with no prior credentials, a small investment, and have a business of your own work. The amount you CAN earn is almost limitless.

AGAINST MLM

In 1980 I wrote a book on Multi-Level Marketing (former name for Network Marketing) and I *barbecued* the entire industry. The title was *The Truth About MLM,* with a skull and crossbones on the cover along with **BEWARE** in large letters followed by several exclamation marks.

Because, I had known and known of so many people who were led like sheep to the slaughterhouse into so many "get rich quick" deals involved with this type of selling. I warned of the pitfalls of MLM; the major ones no longer exist.

In that book, almost 20 years ago, I listed what was necessary to have a SUCCESSFUL Network Marketing company and now, today, starting in the early 1990's there are many. You just have to know not only *what* to look but things to be wary of.

One large red flag (it's also ILLEGAL) is to *front load*—to have people *buy* their position by filling their garage full of products they can only *hope* to sell. Back then, many of the unknowing went bankrupt; they lost their house, their car, their savings and their families.

But, if you deal from your HEAD and not from greed or stupidity, you have a chance. That's what I plan to give you; the best CHANCE there is to be successful in Network Marketing.

Never be SOLD on anything! EVERYBODY has the *best* plan, the *best* company, the *best* product, the best lawyer, doctor, dentist, tax accountant, spouse, etc., And THAT is one of the main ingredients in becoming successful in Network Marketing. You MUST believe in what you are doing,

STATISTICS

I'll not bombard you with statistics, because those aren't always accurate. It depends on who does the survey. Besides, I don't care what is happening in the financial world. My concern is what's going on in MY world—and YOURS!

I remember reading *statistics* when I was only a ten-year old. Statistics said, "America was prosperous and that the average American family was earning $10,000 a year." You understand, this was a long time ago. My father was earning $35 a week BEFORE taxes and I don't want to add or multiply, but that was much less than $10,000 a year.

When the roof leaked from 20 different places in the two-bedroom shack we lived in and we ran out of pots and pans to catch the water, we had to wait maybe three paydays to save the $7.50 for a roll of tar paper. No, I didn't see **my** world as prosperous.

As a fun-loving 21-year-old, there were more *statistics* that said, *"Ski Aspen! Guys, the women are **eight deep** at the bar."* I rushed to Aspen to ski. This was one time statistics were correct; women WERE eight deep at the bar, but MEN were TWENTY deep! So much for statistics.

I don't care how the Network Marketing statistics are documented. Let's make them better. Let's talk about what can be done to help you—NOW!

NO GUARANTEE

I know I've said this a time or two and I'll probably tell it to you a time or two more, but there is NO GUARANTEE in this business! Nor is there a guarantee in ANY business because there are a multitude of things that can go wrong

MOST Network Marketing companies fail the first year. So what? MOST *new companies* FAIL the first year and the **number one reason** is that they make mistakes and they simply MUST have that cash reserve to get through these mistakes.

It makes me smile when people talk about *"get in the company early; get in on the ground floor."* It is often smarter to get into MOST companies AFTER the first year since so many never make it to that 12-month test!

Too, during the first year there will ALWAYS be changes and glitches; it's impossible *not* to have them. There is absolutely NO WAY a company can predict how many distributors they will have in one month, two months, six months.

It is absolutely impossible to store or produce or PREDICT how much PRODUCT you will sell at any given time, certainly not in the first year. And from the corporate standpoint, there will be people to hire, people to fire, people to promote, new methods of telecommunication, new products and maybe a change in the marketing plan.

And, there is NO AMOUNT of advertising where EVERYBODY knows about your particular product, regardless of how unique it is.

I remember a product that I wrote a book about and the company boasted of over 200,000 distributors in two years. Many said "they wish they had gotten in sooner." WHY? It seems that NOW is the best time to get involved.

The glitches are mostly out, the company has a much better idea on what to expect, they have chosen the best people, their pay plan is stabilized and they survived that first year! AND, there are over two hundred MILLION people in the US alone and most of them never heard of this product.

Again, there is never a guarantee of anything

except death and taxes. I remember when dozens of *Mom and Pop* shops in small towns were CLOSED because Wal*Mart moved in. These people had been doing business and earning a living for generations!

And the neighborhood bookstores are fast disappearing because these giant stores with a MILLION books come in and offer discounts, serve *Starbucks coffee,* and are great social gathering places. I love these big stores.

Or some large company comes in and not necessarily a *hostile takeover* situation, but management changes and you get a jerk for a boss or you are laid off or forced into early retirement.

No sir (ma'am) I want to be IN BUSINESS FOR MYSELF, and Network Marketing is the wave of the future. Fact of the matter, it's here NOW! So, jump on the bandwagon, just make certain it's playing the music you like.

FAILURES

There are several reasons why companies fail and Network Marketing companies are no different except, the rules are different.

When you are a State Attorney General and you are making $60,000 a year after graduating from college and then going to law school, it's not an *easy pill to swallow* when you hear of a retired school-teacher, an electrician who lost his business, or some former pizza delivery boy who are all making $400,000 a year working in Network Marketing.

So, they go over your marketing plan with a fine toothed comb and if there is a *hint* of illegality, they move in and shut you down. That happened often a decade and more ago. But now, there are attorneys who specialize in setting up Network Marketing companies and this rarely happens now.

In the back of the *contract* you sign (perhaps printed in small letters because they have a lot to say and limited space to do it) there is a clause that states *"the company has the right to change their compensation plan (even some of their rules) whenever THEY choose"* (or something to that effect). This means that the COMPANY, if their officers so vote, can CHANGE your pay without you having anything to say about it! It happens often.

If this happens *after* you are involved, working and making money ,you have two choices; stay in or leave. I've seen this happen many times over these years with companies who either didn't know what they were doing and had to change their pay plan (rarely in favor of the distributor) or go out of business. Or, the company gets greedy, wants more and ends up causing the entire organization to crumble.

JUMPERS

In every Network Marketing company there are those who do not do well and go over to another company hoping to do better. Most *don't* do better! If they fail in San Francisco, chances are they'll fail in Tallahassee.

With Network Marketing companies, you must work the SYSTEM! Oh, I'll give you ideas, ways, and options to *market* your products or *recruit* new people into your business, but the **system** is always what you must fall back on. WORK THE SYSTEM! Do not try to *reinvent* the wheel.

Network Marketing is WORK, hard work—and that's why I advocate working smart as well as hard. Smart is getting people to call **you**. Hard is going out to them; you must do *both* to prosper

Every *day* I get at least two calls from people wanting me to join this company or that company and each of their companies is the very best. You've been approached, too, haven't you. Time and time again, haven't you? This is when you *must* work from your head and choose wisely. Turn back to Chapter 1 and find out how to choose the *right* company. Even then, there's no guarantee because so many things can go wrong that no *one* person can control.

Network Marketing is no different than any other business—EXCEPT—you can make *more money* in it with such a *small investment and,*

Anyone Can Do It!

Chapter 3
WINNERS AND LOSERS

According to the May 1998 issue of WEALTH BUILDING MAGAZINE, this is a partial list of the top *Direct Sales* organizations in the United States ranked by number of distributors (as of September '98). Now, let me tell you that **THIS IS NOT AN INDICATOR** on how to choose a company.

Many "in the business" say you must have a *consumable* to be successful: NOT necessarily so! *Excel* sells telephones, and *Alpine* markets air purifiers; both excellent, successful companies. There's auto care, dental care, insurance, magnets, kitchen ware, and water filters. A good company has good management, an excellent *proven* product, a pay plan that is "distributor friendly" and they have been around a while. GO with the unique product and a reputable company, you won't make an error.

RANK	# OF DIST.	COMPANY NAME / PRODUCT LINE	START DATE
1	4,000,000	Forever Living / Nutritionals, etc.	1978
2	2,500,000	Amway / Home Care, etc.	1959
3	750,000	Herbalife / Nutritionals, etc.	1980
4	620,000	Excel / Telephone	1988
5	500,000	Sunrider / Nutritionals, etc.	1982

RANK	# OF DIST.	COMPANY NAME / PRODUCT LINE	START DATE
6	500,000	Mary Kay / Cosmetics	1963
7	500,000	Neways / Nutritionals, etc.	1986
8	450,000	Life Plus / Nutritionals, etc.	1970
9	445,000	Avon / Cosmetics	1886
10	400,000	Shaklee / Nutritionals, etc.	1956
11	385,000	Nature's Sunshine / Nutritionals, etc.	1974
12	300,000	Essentially Yours Industries / Nutritionals, etc.	1996
13	220,000	Cell Tech / Nutritionals, etc.	1991
14	220,000	Rexall / Nutritionals, etc.	1990
15	200,000	NSA / Nutritionals, etc.	1970
16	152,000	Enviro-Tech / Auto Care, etc.	1991
17	150,000	Melaleuca / Nutritionals, etc.	1985
18	150,000	Enrich / Nutritionals, etc.	1986
19	135,000	Alpine / Air Purifiers	1989
20	100,000	Nikken / Magnets, etc.	1989
21	100,000	Nu Skin / Skin Care	1984
22	100,000	Nutrition For Life / Nutritionals, etc.	1984
23	100,000	Oxyfresh / Dental Care	1984
24	100,000	Primerica / Insurance	1977
25	100,000	Tupperware / Kitchenware	1951
26	100,000	Equinox / Air & Water Filters	1991

Other seemingly successful companies with less than 100,000 distributors are—**Achievers, Matol, Body Wise, F.I.N.L., IDN, Reliv, Usana, Watkins, Jafra, Nanci, Viva America, Royal Body Care, Market America, Pre-Paid Legal, First Fitness and Fuller Brush.**

The source for the above chart is the combined result of information from our contacts with the individual companies, *Wealth Building Magazine, Money Maker's Monthly* and the *Direct Selling Association.*

Do not misconstrue this list as an endorsement or recommendation of any kind, it's meant to convey my knowledge of their existence only. Go with the company and product you feel most comfortable with and the people you enjoy being around.

The NUMBER of distributors for each of these companies is in constant flux. It is NOT an indication of how well a company is doing. I've seen companies boast of 300,000 or 500,000 distributors and they get greedy and change the marketing plan, up the price on their products, change their product line, the president leaves with the money or they make some stupid error and the company is OVER!

What I want to know about a company is not how many DISTRIBUTORS they list, but . . .

✔ **How many CHECKS they pay out each month.**
✔ **What is the total pay out.**
✔ **How long they've been in business and,**
✔ **How many of their *original distributors* they have since their first few years in the business.**

These are the statistics that never lie!

WHY THEY FAIL

MOST Network Marketing companies the first year because of under-funding. The lack of BACKUP MONEY is number ONE, because there are so many errors that can be made that only money gives you that *staying power* to remedy these errors.

The second reason is a toss up as to whether the corporate officers or the distributors cause the failure. Let's start at the top with the . . .

CORPORATE OFFICERS

Corporate hires incompetent people or they, themselves, are incompetent and can't handle the pressure, and make unwise decisions.

It takes long hours, hard work and *smart* decisions to run a successful organization. Regardless of your product, if you are new at it, you had better be competent or hire those who know how to do it. Or, your company fails.

We would ALL like to help those we love, and several Network Marketing companies are "family run." This doesn't necessarily mean your relative isn't qualified, and it's a thrill to have your brother, son, daughter, or best friend to work with you—but remember, this is BUSINESS and whether it's a loved one or not, your FIRST obligation is to your distributors to give them the best you have.

IF a company starts to *slide,* it takes a substantial bit MORE of hard, smart work AND money to rescue it, and if the slide isn't recognized in time—the outcome is its demise.

UNWISE decisions are common in this business. Many people THINK they are qualified to run a business but they don't quite understand what it takes.

To run ANY business, it takes money, experience, talent and hard, SMART work and of course the **product**! Without competent guidance (and that ever-present need for backup money), it won't work!

GREED, is a large factor among corporate officers (among many people), and when the officers care more about themselves than then do their distributors, *"There's trouble in River City."*

Usually greed sets in when a company (their corporate officers) feel that they *deserve more* for their efforts or so much money comes in so fast that they decide to either "run" with the money and live happily ever after or they "bail out" when the work load gets too much to handle. It happens often and THAT is something none of us can control.

The *positive* in this is that IF you learn the fundamentals of the business, IF you are willing to put in the time and effort and work SMART, there is another CHANCE around the corner with another company with a good product.

It isn't easy to go to your downline distributors and "switch" them, but if the company no longer exists, what choice is there? No, it isn't easy to become a millionaire. If it was, EVERYBODY would be rich!

DISTRIBUTORS CAUSE THE FAILURE

This is the *other side of the coin* for Network Marketing companies failing—dumb or greedy distributors. Let me explain.

If *any* company has 50,000 or 100,000 or more representatives, the chances are high that there will be some *fruit cakes* in the bunch. Since many of the top Network Marketing companies are in health care, these distributors who practice overkill and LIE about or MISREPRESENT their product to make it more appealing to a consumer, and the *company* is held responsible for their actions and gets closed down.

Most NM companies will not allow their distributors to place an ad, make a statement to the newspapers, conduct radio or televison interviews, do their own newsletters or go on the Internet because THEY SAY STUPID THINGS that *could* get the FDA or Attorney General's office or any number of agencies against the company and they are closed down and everyone suffers.

How can you stop this? *You can't!* It's human nature and *Murphy's Law* comes into play often. I've seen (recently) several promising and large NM companies close their doors or lose 75% or more of their distributors because of some dumb move either on the part of corporate or the distributors.

OTHER CAUSES FOR FAILURE

The COMPANY changes their policies. They have fewer meetings, they begin to charge MORE for the product or service, MORE for the sales aids, MORE for company-held meetings and that, ultimately, is *goodbyville* for that company.

IF the company changes their *marketing plan* and *lowers* the commissions of their distributors —*certain death!* This is what usually happens.

Those who were making $20,000, $30,000 or more per month, if cut by as much as half, still stayed in because they had never made that much money before in their lives. So, they *bite the bullet.*

But, the "little folks" who were making $2,000 or $3,000 per month (who usually comprise about 75% of the total distributors) if *their* income is cut in half, they can't live on $1,000 or $1,500 per month, and they *have no choice* other than quit and look elsewhere to survive. It breaks both their pocketbook and their hearts. Yes, it REALLY hurts that group.

Many who quit their regular jobs were counting upon their ability, and the integrity and knowledge of those in charge. But when corporate made the compensation plan change (and they are allowed to do it as is specified on the back of most contracts) these folks couldn't weather the storm, so they left.

And when *they* leave, it isn't long before those who were making the **big** money will be cut even more. It doesn't happen overnight! But it happens. Sometimes it takes four months or six months to catch up, but it WILL, and the company eventually folds.

Again, there is NO GUARANTEE other than death and taxes in ANY company and ALL companies have corporate officers, buyouts, hostile takeovers, changes in management, in policy, etc. There is NO DIFFERENCE in Network Marketing companies. It all depends on just one person—YOU!

BUT, on the *positive* side, If YOU worked hard, learned, trained and have faith in your ability and truly CARE for others, you'll rebound. You'll MAKE it happen. YOU'LL be financially independent. You must take these setbacks in stride and persevere! Remember, if it was easy, we'd ALL be rich.

And don't blame corporate OR these overzealous distributors; neither mean for the company to fail. If it IS the fault of corporate, don't whine about it, just lick your wounds and turn to the next chapter in your book of life. They're only human, and humans have flaws.

Remember that you are an *Independent Distributor* and in business for yourself. They care about you as long as you are making money for them. Like a ball player, when their usefulness to the "team" is over, they are traded, sold, fired and/or forgotten.

Think corporate gives *one thought* about their distributors? Don't be *naive*. **It's a business**! Chances are they'll never see you again because you are out struggling to survive and they are living well.

I have a neighbor, Nolan Ryan, one of the best pitchers ever to play the game of baseball. When he was with the Houston Astros, he had the lowest ERA in the league but he lost too many games. You see, *management* didn't get the players who could hit.

Nolan would have had to pitch a *no-hitte*r to even tie. Sometimes he gave up two or three hits and LOST the game. Sometimes, one hit.

And management let him go to the Texas Rangers where he went on to pitch a few more no hitters and end up in the Baseball Hall of Fame. Management is for management. Smile, be friendly with them but look out for yourself. Nobody else will.

Conversely, if *you* get a better deal, you are gone, too. So *your* loyalty is to *your* business and yourself and your family; their loyalty is to theirs. That's life as it is and not for the dreamers, idealist or the naive.

COMPETITION

No matter WHAT you invent, concoct, formulate or discover, SOMEBODY will try to capitalize on it and sell it cheaper, get it to you faster, promise a better pay plan or offer more amenities and you go for it. It happens every day.

I remember the *Health Rider*, that rowing-type exercise machine that you sit on and exercise using your own body weight. A friend of mine, Lloyd Lambert, invented it. It sold for about $500 and Covert Bailey, best-selling author of *Fit or Fat* was their primary spokesman. The company made a fortune.

Within minutes of the TV campaign, about five *other* machines appeared on the market, some selling for less than $100. The hundred-dollar model wasn't as sturdy or attractive, but it sold and hurt the *Health Rider* sales immeasurably.

This happens in ALL businesses. If somebody else has the *same thing* that is cheaper (or *almost* the same thing) go for IT. That is why I say to choose a NM company who has a UNIQUE product that nobody can copy or sell cheaper, and go with them.

An oft-used example in many NM companies is about Coca Cola. There will always be people who want to *steal* an idea or product by copying what another company has done successfully. The companies who are copied often refer to *Coca Cola* and that fact that *coke* has never been copied, only imitated.

Coke is the number one drink in the world and has been for many years. However, the "other" drinks are selling also and this takes a bite into the coke business. But, they were *so* big that they survived.

Yes, it's sometimes a tough world we live in with competition always nipping at our heels trying to ruin a good thing. We just have to be able to make the right decision and go on with our lives.

Now, let's find out how to give YOU the best CHANCE of making this fascinating business work for you!

Chapter 4
ORGANIZE

This chapter deals with what you NEED to do to be successful in Network Marketing and if you, personally, can't do it, get help from someone who can. I'm about 80% efficient but that's not enough. If you plan to earn BIG money, find someone who is maybe 80% also but their eighty covers your twenty.

You *need* to be (or get) *ORGANIZED*. One of the basic rules for being in business for yourself is TIME MANAGEMENT. Your *time* is your income; try to spend it wisely. No matter how *hard* you work, how *smart* you work, or what you accomplish, you need to **keep records** and this requires doing . . .

PAPERWORK

Regardless of the *number* of people you recruit and sponsor, or how much *product* you sell, it must be properly RECORDED on paper. Make certain you know **exactly** how to do it or all your efforts will be lost. Ask your SPONSOR to teach and assist you with all of it until you are convinced that you know the correct procedure.

This paperwork is as important as a will. If it's

filled out incorrectly, the person you like LEAST might get all of your money. Paying attention to paperwork is essential to getting the "paperwork" everybody loves, *THE CHECKS*.

So, get help. If you are not the type who can keep things in order, enlist help from your spouse, mother, sponsor or somebody. Who knows? You might even recruit your helper to become active in your *downline*. After you learn to correctly fill out the paperwork, you need to keep track of your progress; you need to fully understand about . . .

VOLUME

How much VOLUME do you have? *People* certainly count, but GOOD people count more. I've seen some *lucky* Network Marketers who enrolled only five or ten people and they are making hundreds of thousands of dollars per year. Then, I've seen some who had *thousands* of people and they were making schoolteacher's pay. It isn't "warm bodies" or names, it's the VOLUME of sales that count.

PROSPECTING

Identifying people to recruit for your downline is called PROSPECTING. Just for the heck of it, make a list of everyone YOU KNOW. You'll be surprised to find that you will end up with several *hundred* names—or more. If the Network Marketing company you choose is on the ball, they'll include a sample list in your marketing kit. If not, try this:

When you get up tomorrow morning, have a legal pad and pencil close by to carry with you. If your first move is toward the bathroom, think about talking to your plumber, the salesperson when you go replace your toilet seat, or the people in the grocery where you buy your toilet paper.

When you open your medicine cabinet to get tooth paste, think about talking to your dentist, their assistant, the receptionist. Look at the pills in that cabinet; talk to your doctor, his receptionist, his nurse, people in the waiting room and your pharmacist.

As you put your clothes on, think about talking to the person who sells you pants, a skirt, underwear, shoes. Lost weight? *Gained* weight? How about your seamstress or tailor?

The telephone is ringing. Tell WHOEVER IT IS about your new business. Talk to the telephone repair person, the billing clerk, the person who sells you an additional telephone.

Is it too cold or too warm? Write down the name of your air-conditioning repair person, the meter reader, the secretary at the main office. And on, and on, and on.

I won't walk you to the kitchen or throughout your entire day, I just wanted you to start THINKING. You know, know of, or meet hundreds of people. You pass them, greet them, or visit with them each day. I want you to realize how LIMITLESS your potential is and how endless your list of prospects are.

At work, talk with everyone. At lunch, talk to the waitress. On the way home and passing a toll booth on the expressway, hand the person in that little house a brochure with your name and number on it.

Talk with the mail carrier, clerks at the post office, leave a brochure with them. Get your grass cut? House cleaned? Get the house painted? Speak with them and offer your brochure. Go to the bank? Hand the teller a brochure. Get some plants or garden soil? Leave them a brochure.

You get the idea. You are now in the PEOPLE business, and the more people you talk to the better your CHANCES of being successful in Network Marketing. It is the LEAST EXPENSIVE way I know of to be in business for yourself, and the ONLY limitation you have is your own desire and effort to make it work.

THE THREE-FOOT RULE

This means that when anyone comes within *three feet* of wherever you are, you tell them about what you're marketing. Well, it works for some and scares the daylights out of others. If you want to give yourself the best odds of being successful in Network Marketing, do it. It works. Most of the successful Network Marketers *swear* by it. At least try it.

Look around you. There are truly nice people in the world. If you have a brochure, stick it in their hand as you pass by. They won't hit you or cuss at you.

They might even *call* you if your brochure interests them. The very worst that will happen is that they'll toss it on the ground. Then, somebody else might pick it up and call. EFFORT pays off.

FOLLOW UP

Whew! Is THIS important! After your initial call or contact with a person, call them within a few days and FOLLOW UP! If you don't follow up, you fail. It's that simple. Ask them if they'd like to know more. If they say *yes,* invite them to a meeting or go meet with them at their convenience. They need to know that you are interested enough in what you're doing to find out how they are doing, so FOLLOW UP.

It is a known fact among professional sales people that very few sales are made from an *initial contact* alone. If you ask the top salesperson in any field, "What is your **best** sales technique?" They will reply with two words, "FOLLOW UP!"

TELLING vs. SELLING

A product that I simply love that I feel will make a fortune for all those involved in Network Marketing is . . . **YOUR PRODUCT!** Because, **you** like it, it is unique, **everybody** needs it, it's **easy to explain**, it's *so* unique that cost doesn't matter or it is **affordable** and/or you can get it to them quickly!

Find a product that you need only TELL about,

not sell. The product must sell itself once it's explained and in a short a time as possible.

RECRUIT and SPONSOR

Recruit only, and you'll fail. *Yes*, you have to recruit to get people, just add *sponsor* to that. Recruit and sponsor and you'll win. Here's the difference.

When you *recruit* a person, you just sign them up. *Marines* recruit. They talk to some kid fresh out of high school and tell them all the wondrous things about being a Marine. Those "recruiters" are dressed in their pressed uniforms with all sorts of medals pinned over their left breast pocket. They are just that: Marine ***RECRUITERS***. They do what "recruiters" do; "enroll" the kids, turn them loose, forget about them and they never see the kids again.

But to SPONSOR someone is different. When you *sponsor,* you become responsible for that person. TEACH them the business. Teach them how to teach. Show them the best way to become successful. You SHOW THEM how to go out and sponsor others. Do a good job for them and they'll do one for you.

To do it correctly, help them set an appointment with someone close to them. YOU go along *with* them. YOU do the talking because YOU are their sponsor, their mentor, and YOU know the business. Help them until they get it right.

What you're doing now is TRAINING. You teach that person what **duplication** is. You are building your business by showing them how Network Marketing works. Once they are trained properly and really see it in action, they will go out and do the same thing.

With several of these people in your *downline* (you are their *upline*) you are DOUBLING your own efforts, then redoubling them. You are starting with a PENNY bet on 18 holes and by *training others,* by **duplication**, you will be earning that big money.

MARKETING

Since this is the only way to move your product or service, getting "the word" out to people is necessary. The question is how to do it in the least expensive way and get the best results. Below is a fun example of smart marketing.

About 50 years ago in Louisiana, there was a man named Dudley LeBlanc who began a magnificent marketing campaign for his product called *Hadacol*. I don't even think *Amway* was around then.

He sent over a dozen telephone solicitors into Atlanta, New Orleans, Dallas and Houston. These are supposedly the most difficult southern cities to sell anything new. Each worker was told to sit in their hotel room and call the various pharmacies and grocery stores (before supermarkets even) and ask if they had *Hadacol* in stock. The question always came back; "What's *Hadacol?*" And they were told, not sold.

After a week of making hundreds of calls a day each, they changed cities and began the calling again.

The calls went on for a solid month. Then, in comes a band playing *The Hadacol Boogie* followed by dozens of trucks loaded down with *Hadacol.*

The merchants rushed to get their *allotted* cases of *Hadacol.* Some paid extra *under the table money* to truck drivers to get double and triple the amount LeBlanc set for them. These store owners WANTED the *Hadacol* because they were convinced that their customers wanted it.

I even remember a verse or two of their song.

 "The rooster and the hen were sittin' in the shade.
The hen did the boogie while the rooster layed the egg.
 He did the Hadacol Boogie, the Hadacol Boogie, the Hadacol Boogie makes you Boogie Woogie all the time."

The store owners lined their shelves with lots of *Hadacol* and put up huge signs. When the customers saw this humongous display, they bought *Hadacol.* Everybody loved *Hadacol;* it was said to have cured a multitude of ills. Later it was discovered that it was 33% alcohol. No WONDER it made people feel good; if they drank enough, they all became intoxicated!

I'm not certain of the accuracy of the *Hadacol* scenario, whether my dad told me what was true or what he believed to be true, but I remember that song.

(If we meet, ask me to sing a verse for you). So, whether or not this is exactly how it happened is irrelevant; that's MARKETING.

Another example of marketing I recall hearing about was when the first sardines were introduced to Americans. A company canned PINK sardines. The problem was, pink sardines were very rare whereas WHITE sardines were plentiful.

The public's demand for these pink sardines was so great that the fishermen couldn't catch enough of the smelly little things. A new company emerged and tried to sell WHITE sardines. Consumers wouldn't buy them; they wanted the PINK delicacies.

That's when some marketing genius wrote a powerful message using only eight words on the can of the white sardines:

> # GUARANTEED NOT
> # TO TURN PINK
> # IN THE CAN

Smart marketing, huh?

Chapter 5
MEETINGS and MONEY

I know, you *hate* going to meetings and you have tried and *tried* to get your friends to go to at least one meeting and it is next to impossible.

I, personally, *love* meetings because I like people. And meetings, like them or not, are the LIFEBLOOD of every Network Marketing company. If you don't enjoy meetings, **learn** to enjoy them because they are the very best way to increase your business. Period.

You LEARN at meetings, and learning is what is foremost in this business. You learn from the person conducting the meeting and you learn from others present at the meeting. Then you begin trying to get your friends and prospects to a meeting.

GETTING FRIENDS to MEETINGS

Most people hate being SOLD anything. Also, most people have been to a meeting involving selling something and they will use *every excuse* in the world NOT to go with you. The second you tell them it's an "opportunity" meeting, an *invisible wall* appears that even *Superman* can't break through. Most have heard of an "opportunity" meeting and they don't want an *opportunity,* so PLEASE don't call it that.

People LIE to **not** go to an "opportunity" meeting with their best friends. They just know you're going to try to get them to sell make-up, soap, vitamins, floor polish, invest in a bank in the Cayman Islands, or go in with them in a timeshare condo with 50 others for your one week per year in Afghanistan. If they've lived long enough, chances are they have been very disappointed by one company or another and they want no part of any MEETING.

Even if they (finally) agree to have you pick them up at their home, there have been instances where the ENTIRE family turns out all the lights and lies *face down on the floor* afraid to breathe, with hopes that you stop ringing their doorbell or pounding on their door. They'll make up a good lie for you in the morning once they've had time to think about it.

More friendships have been broken by a person in Network Marketing who uses the WRONG approach to get friends to a meeting than anything in the world (other than relatives acting as bone-pickers when a will is read).

So, find the *best way you can think of* to invite a friend to a meeting. But, please *don't deceive* them pretending you're inviting them out to eat or to a movie. I've found that the best approach is to ask them to accompany you to the meeting as a personal favor to you as you'd rather not go alone.

If you take but one new person a week to a

meeting for one year, your chances of becoming successful in Network Marketing is almost guaranteed. You have put the odds in your favor.

When you bring a guest, even if you've heard the same presentation a *thousand* times, still *look* as interested as if it were your first time. If you get up, or move around, or become seemingly bored, so will your guest. Remember this is the FIRST DATE. Be at your very best and it will increase the odds of your guest responding favorably.

If your guest is interested in making money, keep them there *after* the main meeting and explain the compensation plan. I'd NEVER recommend you talk money unless your guest is really interested. First, talk PRODUCT, friendships, and fun. Most people can use a few new friends and everybody likes fun.

If you invite (or take) your new guest to a FUN meeting, that guest will bring a new guest with them the *following* week. This is a great method to create your *downline* organization and build your business.

Getting a new person to a meeting every week is the tough part. Persistence pays off. Work on several people each week to improve your odds. I would choose the approach that fits your personality. Here are a few ideas:

Friend #1 Tom: *"I just learned of a terrific new company that I'm considering being a part of. I value your opinion and I want you to hear what they say and have you advise me."* (This approach has been used often, but it still works.)

Let's say you just delivered the above "opinion pitch" to a friend. If they've been an adult for five or so years, chances are they've heard it before. Typical reply:

Friend #2 John: *"If this is one of those stupid **pyramid** deals, don't do this to me. Don't drag me in with you."* (This is where you "sort of" level with him.)

Friend #1 Tom: *"I'm already IN it. (No need to lie, he's on to you) and I really and truly LIKE it. You're my friend. I've gone several places with you that I didn't want to go, so all I'm asking is that you tell me what you think."* (Press a little. You believe in what you're doing.)

It's no big deal among friends to call in a *marker.* If you've been friends long enough, you each owe the other for a bad date, bad vacation, bad meal, bad movie, bad *something.* Be truthful. But, be creative and find a way to drag them to that meeting. You're clever and innovative, think of a way. Straightforward honesty, I've found, is the best method for everything.

If it's an acquaintance, tell them about the product and/or the compensation plan, invite them to dinner or drink before the meeting. Agree to pick them up to (almost) assure that they will be at the meeting.

If it's a friend, relative or a loved one, you *owe* it to them to share your good fortune, to help them find something that might change their lives for the better. If you **believe** in what you're doing, so will they.

GOOD MEETINGS vs BAD MEETINGS

When someone conducts a few bad meetings, attendance drops. Meetings should not last longer than ONE HOUR at the most, and they should start on time. If you want to stay longer, there will always be little "bunches" of people at a table or in the corner of the room talking about something. Ease on over and eavesdrop, you might learn something interesting.

If that person conducting the meeting cannot drive their PRODUCT INFORMATION across in 60 minutes or less, find another meeting. If you have a guest who wants to *learn* about the product, do not take them to a meeting where they will be sold or brainwashed. Often, on bad meetings, the person conducting the meeting either reads information, or becomes so enamored with their own voice that they lull you to sleep.

Meetings have to be both informative and fun. If you're new in the business, have your sponsor, mentor or favorite *upline* help you with that person you bring to the meeting. But again, only to inform not sell.

Sing the praises of both the product and the company. Introduce your guest to some people you know and like. Make them feel important and smile a lot. Make that meeting fun.

If the meeting coordinator is not to your liking or the meeting is too lengthy, **DO NOT WASTE A PROSPECT BY TAKING THEM THERE**! Tell them about the plan yourself or get your mentor to do it. Be candid with your mentor and tell them if you feel the meeting is too long or too boring. It's business. Good meetings are the best way to sponsor new people.

How am I such an authority on meetings? I've been a guest speaker at least 5,000 times at both good and bad meetings; I know a good one from a bad one. I've given both. I've spoken before the Lions, Rotary, Kiwanis, Chambers of Commerce, breakfast clubs, a multitude of book stores, singles groups, hearing aid seminar, truckers, oilfield roughnecks, garden clubs, greens keepers, bird watchers, the 82nd Airborne, nurses conventions, horticultural groups, teacher's outings and a funeral director's convention.

HOME MEETINGS

What if you are first in your area and there are *no* meetings? Begin with your home meeting. Invite friends and neighbors and family to a "gathering" at your home. Don't know much? Learn. Remember, if you don't know what you're talking about, how can you explain it to others?

When you learn what you're talking about, have that home meeting of six or eight or how many you can comfortably seat, and share your enthusiasm and knowledge with them. It has to begin somewhere, and home meetings can be easier to get people to attend. They're your friends, they can easily walk or drive to your home. If you're new in the business, have your sponsor conduct the meeting.

Whether you serve refreshments, cookies or snacks is up to you. Try to have the kids out of the house, and either put your telephone on an answer machine (first ring) or pull out the plug. You need to be able to focus your attention on your subject as you speak. *And*, you need *their* UNDIVIDED attention.

REGIONAL MEETINGS and CONVENTIONS

Network Marketing companies have regional meetings to make certain that any bad *local* meetings are buffered by professional ones. Take your new prospects to these. This is part of the company's support system to help their distributors.

Conventions are the **best** meetings to attend. If you can entice a person you want to sponsor to a *convention*, they WILL be impressed.

The speakers are usually chosen for their ability to communicate and they are usually the *elite* of the company. They are the ones who know how to make things happen. You can learn from them.

I attended an absolutely fantastic convention meeting with a new company where the officers and just about everyone present were all splendid; friendly, caring, my kind of people.

They tried to get only the big money earners to speak but they also went for the good speakers. Their "breakout sessions" where they trained people, had the tops in their respective fields.

Most companies "honor" their top income

producers but this doesn't qualify that top earner to speak; some are horrid communicators. I say give them plaques, cash bonuses, trips, or new cars but *let the ones who speak well,* **speak!**

Yes, **good** meetings are powerful and great for getting new people involved. There's excitement—electricity—in a good meeting and excitement is contagious. Bad meetings only run people off; too many bad meetings and NOBODY attends!

NEW FRIENDS

I have met *many* truly wonderful people while researching this Network Marketing business. They are all *"so alive"* and always doing things. I have made so many new friends and so will you.

It's like one huge club, and when they have large meetings, it reminds me of a high school reunion. I dedicated my book to Network Marketers from everywhere!

Because of my first book, and now this one, I have become a part of a large Network Marketing *"family."* My books have helped change the lives of many, and I feel really good about myself because of it.

I actually LOVE to sit around a table of Network Marketing people and listen to their enthusiasm about their products or services.

Some are rich and some aren't. There isn't a class barrier of any kind, although their are *cliques,* the same as in any school, club, etc. The BIG money earners know each other and the *little* money earners know (or know OF) the ones who make a bunch.

The big money folks are announced at the conventions and are featured in the monthly magazine or newsletter. It's the same as the guy in school who scores the most touchdowns or the gal who is selected as homecoming queen. Want to be known? Want to be a winner? Succeed, too!

Do I LIKE Network Marketing? **I LOVE it!** Because of the people in it and because if you do it wisely, you truly CAN change your financial life. I say TRY Network Marketing; mingle with those who *are making things happen,* having fun and making money together under a common cause.

MONEY:
EARN $500 to $1,000 PER MONTH

If your present job has a *frozen* income, there's a place for you in Network Marketing. A PART TIME home-based business is an excellent way to earn a *little* more money for those who enjoy their *regular* job.

Find a *product* in a Network Marketing company that you like, put as little as 10 to 12 hours a week working smart, and you *could* bring home that extra $500 to $1,000 per month within a few months.

Doesn't seem like much? *Hey!* That's up to you. Set your own goals. Put in another several hours and DOUBLE that, maybe. It costs so very little to try.

It's simply amazing how the *amount you earn* doing anything is almost *directly related* to the amount of *effort* you put into it. If you'll notice, those who work the hardest and the smartest always seem to have the most. They're often not necessarily the smartest people either, are they? *Anybody can do it!*

B-I-G MONEY

I can remember when I won $1,200 gambling at a casino in the Bahamas; it was about 1954 I think. That, then, to me, was big money.

Later, the few years I worked as a commercial diver when I got a job retrieving guided missiles for the government I earned $3,000 a week—now THAT was big money. (I didn't make that *every* week.)

Another time I invested in an apartment building and sold it in about a month. The difference was $75,000. Now, THAT was big money. I didn't do that often either.

In Network Marketing, I know people who are making $50,000 and $75,000 a MONTH—month after month. Now, THIS is big money. I can't list their *names,* but know that there are a great many doing it now and more doing it each day. Yes, . . .

Anyone Can Do It!

Chapter 6
WORKING SMART

As I said a time (or two) before, I think the OLD way—alone—is tough to work and the reason why so many do not even *attempt* Network Marketing.

You see, the word *"marketing"* means *"selling"* something and many people don't want to, don't know how to, or just can't SELL! Certain personalities are just not conducive to selling anything. So, MY methods are new—and they WORK!

MY METHODS

I have devised methods that get people coming to YOU, calling YOU to find out about BUYING something that you happen to have; you don't SELL, you simply TELL them about it.

By using this method, all you need to do is LEARN what you're going to TELL them about, then tell them and they buy it. It puts *Network Marketing* in a new light. It opens the door for many who shied away from it in the past. It's SMART marketing.

The industry of Network Marketing truly IS fascinating; it has made MORE millionaires in the past decade than any business—even counting the enormous salaries athletes are getting paid, and this includes winners of the state lotteries. But, like most other things, we remember the BAD and rarely the good. It's our nature.

For instance, most people feel an *author* is someone who is bright. And most people *think* that being an author is something special. The fact is, *most* authors are starving, and have other jobs in order to survive.

Years ago I recall reading in one newspaper or other that of the 500 *lowest* paying jobs, number 500 was a *migrant farm worker,* and number 499 was a *freelance author!* For now, forget that statistic.

Since I write books, I'm an author. I want the majority to feel that authors ARE important, that they ARE bright, that they ARE special. It just turns the table on the bad rap that Network Marketers have because it's THESE people who are special, yet when you tell people you are in Network Marketing—they flee as if you just announced that you escaped quarantine from a Yellow Fever ward.

So, let's turn it around, you *and* me—**together!** Let's take advantage of the opportunity and make Network Marketing the honored profession it should be and make YOU a NEW MILLIONAIRE!

USE THE BOOK

Other than the information you get from *reading* this book, you can start *selling* it, *giving* it away, or using it as an *incentive* for people to buy your particular product—whatever it is.

Simply GET IT TO as many people as you can whom you feel would like to be in business for themselves. Let IT sell them on the business; let it TELL them what this business is all about.

If, after reading this book, they don't call you for more information on your particular NM company, they are either already rich or they are really stupid. You can work with the rich but you simply cannot work with dumb.

That reminds me of a tale I read about Winston Churchill, the able and witty former Prime Minister of England.

It seems he was at a party one evening and drinking a bit heavily. Some lady came up and openly chastised him.

"Winston, you are drunk!" she said in a voice that almost everyone could hear.

Churchill replied in an equally boisterous tone. *"And you, madam, are ugly. In the morning, I shall be sober but you will **still** be ugly!"*

I'm not certain where that fits in here but it's funny and it could be the same as a dumb person who has either no common sense, no ambition, and will waste your time. Drunk is for the night, but *stupid* is forever. Now, let me tell you what this book can do for you and how it can help make you rich!

RADIO SHOWS

There are *thousands* of talk shows each day with hosts who *hunger* for new material. They oftentimes need upwards of 1,000 topics per year if they have a one-hour show each day, and they LIKE controversial subjects. Network Marketing IS a subject most can relate to and many will listen to.

I have been on the radio at least 100 times in the past 8 months because of a book I had written titled LOSE FAT WHILE YOU SLEEP. The subtitle was NO Diets, NO drugs, NO exercise.

Whenever a station was called for an interview, mostly *all* loved the title and booked me for a 10 to 60-minute show that brought literally thousands of listeners clamoring to find out how to get a FREE book.

That's what I told them: *"Want to find out how to get a FREE book?"* And, the book WAS free IF they bought the miracle weight-loss product. In the BACK of the book was a sticker with YOUR telephone # *(you can get 500 for about four bucks)* and many passed the book on to a friend (I told them to do so in the book) and the FRIEND called for product.

YOU can do the same with THIS book on Network Marketing. Just, *first*, LEARN about your product and your company. MANY people *"out there"* want more money. MANY people *"out there"* want a home-based business. And, YOU can tell them about it and interest them in YOUR business.

Hopefully you chose the RIGHT product, company and compensation plan on your own or did so after reading this book, so you can guide these "needing" folk correctly.

Think this won't work? It WILL! It HAS worked hundreds of times. One time, after but a 45-minute talk show in I did in Ohio, a young lady got over *300 calls* and signed up 81 NEW distributors in *three weeks*.

Another time in Kingston, Ontario (Canada) 65 people braved a *blizzard* to come to a meeting and receive a *free book*. Too expensive, you say? NOT when you sell product with each book you give away and enroll new distributors.

Think it's worth five dollars to get an interested couple to a meeting with other interested couples without begging, threatening or lying to them? Trust the fact, it's cheap!

I could give you *hundreds* of success stories with these radio spots. This alone has changed the entire Network Marketing industry. *Nobody in the past* has been able to solve the dilemma of getting people to a meeting, getting people to ask YOU about your product or your business without promising them free FOOD or DRINK.

You read the chapter before this one on meetings. It's true, isn't it? It is tough work to get even *friends and relatives* to attend a meeting. So, work on strangers; they're easier to sell anyway.

These talk shows that are EVERYWHERE have hosts who HUNT for new material daily; some as many as four programs for one or two hours times 300+ days or 1,200 spots for as many as 2,000 topics.

A book on Network Marketing is certainly *evocative* because SO MANY people want to make big money and start a business of their own. And many have FAILED at Network Marketing and they (the listeners) want to get their darts ready for anyone who is positive about a business (or businesses) where *they* have failed. Hence, a good show for the station.

Best of all, it's the way to get YOUR product advertised FREE. All YOU have to do is stay at home, and answer the calls, and TELL the caller about it. You have them In YOUR backyard, on YOUR turf, in YOUR arena. This is the plan:

◆ Find a local talk show in your city or a city nearby, send them a copy of my book along with my PROFILE and I'LL do the show for you.

◆ Call me to make certain I'm still alive. I'll send you some of my PROFILE'S.

◆ Then, a week later, CALL the station and TALK to the D.J. (or program director), tell them how funny, smart, and witty I am (in other words, LIE), just get me ON THAT SHOW. It costs you NOTHING!

◆ Then, you call me or two or give me the number of the station who has agreed to book me and I'll set up a time ANY time, ANYwhere.

I've done shows from my cell phone, on my way to a meeting, at the airport, in the dentist office, on the golf course—even in the bathroom.

◆ When I get on the show and talk about MY BOOK

and about NETWORK MARKETING, I never mention a product. I just talk about the book, how ANYONE can start a home-based business for peanuts and how they can get a FREE copy of the book to tell them how to do it, and I give YOUR number! I don't have to personally know you, your product nor your company but the subject is Network Marketing. This is *the hook*.

AFTER the show (and a few times during it) I tell them how they can **find out** how to get a **free copy** of THE NEW MILLIONAIRES and I give them YOUR telephone number.

When the people call—and they WILL—and ask for the FREE BOOK, you tell them something like, *"Well, the book sells for $10 but I'll send you one for only $5. AFTER you read it, if you'll send it back, I'll refund the $5."* Or, *"I'll hand you a **free** copy of the book if you will be able to spend an hour or so with me this coming (Thursday, Friday, etc. evening) in a small gathering."*

Do you see what this is doing? It's getting them to come to YOU, at YOUR convenience, in YOUR back yard, so you can explain YOUR Network Marketing plan to them. It's worked a few hundred times, and it works EVERY time. It's never missed and NOBODY is offended.

This is what's happening. You are advertising free and your only expense is maybe the $5 you pay for the book (wholesale for a case price). AND, you violate NO RULES in your company because you aren't advertising THEIR product; I am advertising MY book! Everyone profits.

Trust the fact, it is far EASIER than having to

drive to THEIR house, taking up YOUR time in an atmosphere that might not be ideal. At YOUR meeting place, there will be NO kids running around, NO telephone to ring, NO television to compete with and NO hostile spouse who doesn't believe in one of those "pyramid things."

People are drawn to FREE like a shark to blood. They BELIEVE you when it's written in a book. It gives you AND Network Marketing credibility.

EVERYBODY has an audio tape with some voice (not often a good voice) telling you about something or other. I must have a hundred or more tapes *lying around* that were sent to me that I just do NOT listen to. You do, too, don't you?

I'm not throwing a *rotten tomato* at audio or video tapes, because they are *necessary* for training, they are *great* for someone telling about your product who knows what they're talking about but, trust the fact, the BOOK has more credibility. I can't explain why, it just does.

Remember my radio show In Kingston, Ontario? The one where I was able to drag 65 Canadians to a meeting in a blizzard with the promise of a FREE book? EVERY ONE of them bought at least one bottle of a weight loss product my friend was selling.

On another radio show in Saskatoon, Saskatchewan, a NM friend logged over 250 calls after *one* 30-minute radio broadcast and this scenario has repeated itself time and time again across the United States and Canada.

I have a friend, a health practitioner in California, who has a weekly one hour show she advertises over and she has had me do the program at least a dozen times in the past several months. She reaches thousands of listeners a week and she is making B-I-G money. It is the *new*, SMART way to Network Market and coupled with the *old* way, it can't miss.

Yes, get them to come to YOU and you only need TELL them about whatever it is you're trying to market. And, after they read the book you are training them in the right way because this book pulls no punches and tells them what to expect.

They are also able to QUALIFY THEMSELVES from this book and (again) I don't know why, but they BELIEVE an author and they LISTEN when it is in book form. It gets you qualified people who want to make money and it saves you TIME.

And, there's no need to invest a LOT of money to try. The books are $10 apiece, but $8 each for 10; $7 each for 25; $6 each for 50 and for a case of 100 books, they are only $5 each and we pay shipping and taxes.

Perhaps you're wondering, *"How can this guy promise his time to so many?"*

Good question and easy to answer. Because, *woefully*, MOST of you reading this book are in the category of those who WATCH things happen. If you read this book and believe it, you now know WHAT'S happening and all it takes—now—is for YOU get off your lazy rear and MAKE things happen!

So, do you SEE what I'm doing? I'm giving you ammunition to MAKE things happen for yourself and if you want to use ME, we can do it together. Last year I sold over 240,000 of my books this way alone. That interprets to being 240,000 CALLS from people who wanted to learn more about a product Network Marketers (like yourself) were selling.

I am, in a fashion, Network Marketing my books and at the same time making YOU money and bringing new HOPE to others who have a regular job with NO HOPE of ever getting rich. Together, you and I, WE can bring hope to these people and still profit ourselves. What a truly WONDERFUL way to earn money and help others!

I have a brochure that I hand out titled, WAYS FOR YOU TO HELP ME, HELP YOU. It tells in detail how each of these methods I mention in this chapter work. It truly IS the smart way and you needn't be a salesperson to do it. It works, folks. It works well, and EVERYONE benefits.

It works because I am a THIRD party who does not belong to your company nor sell your product. Your COMPANY cannot object because YOU are not on the air promising things that aren't, and I don't even have to *mention* the company nor the product, just an *opportunity* in Network Marketing

Unashamedly speaking, I'm GOOD at what I do. I have a strong voice, I'm passionate about Network Marketing and I know how to get people's interest. TRY it with ONE station. Buy ONE book, call me and let's try. There's no reason to buy a slug of books to TRY. Do it ONLY when you GET these calls.

TV SHOWS

Even with *five thousand* channels (it seems) televison is still, by far, the best and fastest way to get a message across to people. Big companies pay MILLIONS of dollars for a one-minute ad during the Super Bowl or the Academy Awards IF a spot is available. Of course, *you* can't do that.

But TRY! Call *any* local TV station and tell them about my book and see if they will have me on. Do NOT mention that you are selling a product, just that I'm a friend who wrote a book about a home based business and I am funny, smart, charming (lie again and again; it's for a good cause) but get me on televison—if you can—and I'll do the same as I did on the radio for you.

The main problem(s) with televison is that they want to *charge* for time but if you convince them that my appearance will attract a listening audience for them, they *might* do it. It's worth a phone call.

The other problem is that *I have to be there* in the studio, and this should be done when I'm going to be in your town anyway conducting a meeting. One group had a meeting planned a month ahead but since nobody knows me (or cares) they drew maybe 50 people. With one 7-minute TV spot, we had over seven HUNDRED! Yes, televison is powerful.

I'LL DO YOUR MEETING

Call me, plug me into YOUR MEETING, and I'll give 8 or 10 or 15 minutes of information to YOUR group that you gathered from the radio ad on the wonders and opportunity of Network Marketing.

Either the people there got my book FREE from you (you bought them) or they are getting them that evening. Do you see, I'M doing the meeting FOR you. It gives you time to observe their reactions to what I say and make your plan on how to close them.

If they heard me on the radio and called you, they will be thrilled that "an author" is talking only to them. Sounds egomaniacal on my part, I know, but I'm telling you fact! I am *not* important, I am *not* special, but if people THINK I'm special, it gets the job done.

STORES

I know that you or some of those in your downline go to the beauty parlor, veterinary clinic, a doctor, dentist, or have a friend with a small business. **Get this book in those places!** I have some small plastic stands that sell for $5 each I'll sell to you (or get your own) that holds 5 or 6 books.

Put YOUR STICKER in the back of the book with YOUR telephone number on it, pay the store $4 for selling the book and wait. You make a buck a book (no big deal) but with YOUR sticker in the back of that book, the percentage of CALLS that people have gotten is ... 20 books out (4 in 5 stores or 5 in 4 stores) and they get NINE CALLS A WEEK from someone who bought the book! Then, TELL them about your product or service.

> A good move to save you money is to get 3 or 4 people together and buy in QUANTITY.

ANOTHER (OVERLOOKED) MARKET

Years ago, when my *How Not to Be Lonely* book (that changed my financial life forever) was hot off the press, I had two of the strongest motivating factors in the world—HUNGER and LOSS OF DIGNITY!

No publisher would take my book. All said, *"You have no relevant credentials."* I was not a psychologist, psychiatrist or a counselor. I tried for more than *two years* to find an agent or a publisher but none thought my book was worthy. So I published it myself.

Even then, I couldn't get a distributor to put the books in book stores; that took three *years.* So, WHERE could I sell my book? **I worked the organizations**. Why can't you do the same?

I called every social, civic and business club within driving distance from my home and I talked to them. They love speakers on *any* subject. If you have a topic to speak about, call these clubs and book yourself. Get their addresses from a book you can get FREE from your local Chamber of Commerce.

If you're afraid, don't be. Even if you're a

beginning speaker, as long as you have a subject of interest, they'll accept you. It is a ripe market for telling about your product. If you can't do it, get someone in your downline or upline to do it and you go along with them to do the *grunt* work (haul books, sell books and take in the money).

Not a good way to market anything, you say? Too hard to do? I sold more than 100,000 books in 12 months at ten bucks each (*that's one MILLION dollars in book sales*) on this circuit of **local** clubs and organizations. I hung in there like a *pit bull*.

The more experience I got, the better speaker I became. My crowds got larger and I sold more books. You can do it too. Persevere! I made upwards of 600 speeches that first year to **anyone who would listen**—and I sold books.

For three years running I didn't see my house during daylight hours—I was up before light and home way after dark—weekdays, weekends, holidays, *every* day. Even Christmas and New Year, I hired out as a comedian (of sorts) to parties and sold books.

I talked to any group that had warm bodies present: Lions, Rotary, Kiwanis, church groups, luncheon clubs, Chambers of Commerce, business clubs, singles organizations—ANYONE who would book me—and I sold books.

I was frightened (*for the first time in my life*) because I was past 50, broke, and I OWED almost a million dollars. Everything went; the 31 foot Wellcraft cruiser, the gold Mercedes, finally my beautiful town home on the water. Soon after—*my dignity*.

But, I can only *imagine* what I could have made if I had a *product* or a *business* to sell—something that they bought month, after month, after month. YOU, have it!

AARP GROUPS

This is an **excellent** market to pursue and you don't have to be over 50 to do it. They even *feed* you. Many of these folks were retired before they were ready to retire. So, Network Marketing with a great product and a low cost to get in would certainly interest many. If you jut get *one* in the group and you help them, you could get the *entire organization*!

ALL of these organizations meet weekly, or semi-monthly, or monthly, and they ALL need speakers. It takes effort, but its fun. And, you get 50 or 60 or 80 people (or more) to hear "your story" at one time. Sell them books for $10 (that you get for $5) and make a few hundred for your effort.

And if YOU are afraid to speak or stutter like Mel Tillis (*when he's not signing*), find someone in your downline who will do it and again go along with them and at least carry books; make yourself useful and have fun doing it.

Chapter 7
LISTEN TO THE EXPERTS

I have interviewed at least **two hundred** *experts* in this business; people who make from several hundred thousand a year to over a million dollars a year and more. I took information from each and put it all in one chapter. Read it, please!

It's the "old" way but it's the *certain* way, and you NEED what these people say in order to be successful in Network Marketing. Coupled with my *new* methods, you simply cannot miss!

The experts concur: If you want to be successful in Network Marketing you MUST work a *system.* Distributors are constantly trying to design their *own* system and this almost always leads to confusion and frustration within an organization.

Consistency and repetition ultimately leads to **duplication,** the basis of ALL successful Network Marketing plans. Want a plan? Want some guidelines to become successful? Read the following carefully, then . . . *memorize* it.

❏ **BELIEF** in your products, your company, Network Marketing and yourself. When you have this belief, it's easy to share your company with others. Ask yourself. *Is this a product I would use and share with others? Do I believe in Network Marketing as a legitimate business? Do I believe that I can be a success in this company?"*

❏ **COMMITMENT** is the key word. Do whatever it takes to get the job done.

❏ **URGENCY** means push the throttle to the floor to build your business. You *must* have a high level of enthusiasm for an extended period of time so the people around you will feel your energy—your *electricity*—and want to become a part of it.

❏ **SET YOUR GOALS:** Write them down and read them daily. Dream, and dream BIG! Know the REASONS you want to achieve these goals, WHEN you want to achieve these goals, and HOW you plan to do it. Be specific! It is also important for you to frequently REVIEW these goals.

❏ **DUPLICATION:** This is a word that cannot be overused in Network Marketing. It is **impossible** to succeed alone. Success comes in abundance when you learn the art of duplication. It is important to have a *system* **for building a system** that is easily *duplicatable.*

One of the first things to learn in this business is **Never do anything other people can't copy!** Have a simple plan, one that everyone can follow, and repeat that plan (that system) over and over and over.

❏ **MAKE A LIST:** Have someone you just sponsored list 20 of the *most important* people in their life, never prejudging anyone. (YOU do the same when you first start). From that list of 20 names, select the **top five** prospects and set an appointment with each for a *two–on–one* presentation or a *three–way* call.

For the presentation, the upline (or mentor) conducts it while you observe. These beginning five prospects are the KEYS to your business. If it's a three–way call, the upline still makes the presentation to the prospect and you listen.

Two things are happening: First, the upline will be more successful with the prospect because they know the system. Second, you are being trained. Repeat this procedure until you feel confident to conduct a presentation yourself. Now, what about the remaining 15 prospects from that list?

Invite the remaining 15 people to an in-home presentation where the upline looks for the prospects who have *fire in their eyes*, those who recognize the opportunity before them. These potential prospects become the new recruits and the process starts over again, with the former new distributor being the mentor/presenter. This is **DUPLICATION**!

AFTER you finish with the original 20-people,

create an *Organic Prospect List* of maybe 200 (neighbors, friends, relatives, acquaintances across the United States or anywhere in the world). Each week, select *ten names* from the list and make these your contact people for the week.

Every week add *five names* to the list, people you meet just walking through life. And remember, NEVER prejudge. You never know who will or who won't be your next leader. If you have but ten new distributors using the same system, after ten weeks you, personally, would have contacted 100 people and if the distributors you trained were trained well, they will have contacted a THOUSAND people! **THIS IS DUPLICATION!** This is the BIG SECRET of what makes Network Marketing work!

❑ **A FOLLOW-UP SYSTEM:** Develop a follow-up system for your new distributors and for your retail customers. Send them a tape, a piece of literature, etc., for a specific period of time on a regular basis.

This will introduce them to the entire product line a product at a time, or to the business opportunity. It is a very effective *drip system* that leads to building great business relationships as well as bringing steady increases and consistency to your sales. People want to know that you care.

❑ **A SUPPORT TEAM:** What a fun way to do business. Everyone needs a friend, a cheerleader, a *confidante* in the business. When you are UP, it's great to be recognized, and when you're DOWN, you'll welcome support. Develop a team of four or five people and create a Support Team.

❏ **TEAMWORK:** *Everyone working together* will accomplish more. Be a leader in your business. Remember, you are working WITH your distributors not FOR them. Everyone is in business FOR themselves, but not BY themselves. Understanding that each person has different talents allow your distributors to use *their* talents; you will all benefit. If you find a leader, *let them lead!*

❏ **FOCUS:** It's like MAGIC, and gives you a chance for great success in everything you do, and *especially* in Network Marketing. Focus on ONE company. Rarely can you work two or more successfully. There ARE exceptions, of course. If want to build confidence in your distributors, the best way to destroy it is to become the mayor, sheriff, fire chief and postmaster.

❏ **VISION:** This is the initial step to take in creating the business to which you aspire. Tell your distributors, "*If you could only see what I see.*" Remember Helen Keller? She said, "*The most pathetic person in the world is someone who has sight but no vision.*"

Network Marketing has given financial security

to so many. And you, as a leader, can make a positive difference in many lives and represents all that is good about democracy. It gives the average person the *opportunity* or *freedom* to pursue their dreams and to be the best they possibly can be.

This is not a *free lunch* program. It's an opportunity to build an organization with hard work and dedication and make money to whatever heights you can imagine.

Network Marketing contains the two major principles of financial success. The people that I know who are financially successful incorporate these two principles: The first is OWNERSHIP. Successful people own common stocks, real estate, and natural resources.

The second of the principles is LEVERAGE OF DUPLICATION. The successful ones have found a way to *leverage* their money or finances and/or to leverage and duplicate their time. Where else can you find an opportunity to incorporate the above principles with unlimited potential and, for all practical purposes, have little capital expenditure which equates to very little financial risk?

Network Marketing is truly the answer. It empowers you with ownership, freedom, and the success systems in place to have the best chance for a successful experience. The two main ingredients you must contribute is: ENTHUSIASM and ACTION.

Just a few nights ago a friend invited me to a meeting to hear the top money earner in this particular company give a speech. Over the years I must have heard at least several hundred speakers but I still go now and then if I hear someone is really good.

The speaker's name was Bob Giddens. He was dressed in sport coat and tie, he started his meeting ON TIME and the room (he knew) would *barely* be large enough to handle the expected crowd. He was pleasant and friendly, but no big jokes; he was there for business.

The meeting lasted a little over an hour. He *held* the audience (including me) in the palm of his hand as he moved from product to money to a few tips on how to *work* the business.

"Don't waste time," he said. *"My first four days in the business I signed up 4 people. The fifth day I was with a friend who asked how I was doing. I told him that I was doing great—that I had signed up four people. He knows I don't lie and he joined.*

"A month later each of the first four I signed up were out. One signed up and paid the registration fee, and never worked the business. The second bought some product but got a new job and moved. The third has done nothing and I forget what happened to the fourth. I now had just ONE of the original five—my friend. That one friend has made me about a half million dollars!

*"Suppose I had taken a month to talk with those first four people and the fifth week I spoke with my friend who asked how I was doing? I would have truthfully had to say **lousy,** and chances are high that*

he would have not signed.

*"Do you see what I'm saying? Work fast and work NOW! Don't wait! Don't make excuses as to why you **can't** begin work now! As Pete said in the beginning of this book, If you think you can—or think you can't—you're right!"*

Bob showed his income on a chalk board. He wasn't smug about it. He had worked for the company five years and he told us he worked hard.

His first year he earned $99,000 (I didn't copy this exactly but this is what I recall). His second year was about $385,000, and his third year was over $600,000. His fourth year he earned over $955,000 and his fifth year he dropped a bit below $900,000. This year, if things continue, he'll make well over a million dollars!

ANOTHER EXPERT GIVES ADVICE

❏ **LISTEN:** Be open minded so you are TEACHABLE. You have to LEARN the business and then be able to TEACH the business to others. Your goal is to SPONSOR and to DUPLICATE yourself.

❏ **LEARN:** Daily self-development can start with listening to 15 minutes of training tapes, meditating, praying, exercising, or reading to develop your mind, body and soul. Do these things EVERY DAY! You'll become more productive, have more self-confidence, and have a greater sense of purpose. Magical things will start to happen.

❏ **WORK BEYOND YOUR COMFORT ZONE:** When you grow PERSONALLY, your network grows. Anything that you can do to get out of that COMFORT ZONE will make you a stronger and better person. Thus, you're growth will increase exponentially and so will your business.

SUCCESS doesn't come from changing the *people* in your organization. Nor does it come from changing your *sponsorship line or company*; success comes when YOU change.

Change your bad habits and adopt new, good habits. You might have to work at it, but if you really want a growing, dynamic, empowering organization, YOU have to actually become a growing, dynamic, empowering person.

"Here are the tools I recommend: Let's suppose you have almost no money. How do you begin? You begin by listening with your ears, seeing what's going on with your eyes, and developing a positive attitude. If you don't believe in yourself, who will?

❏ **POSITIVE ATTITUDE:** Have the **desire,** and dream of a better lifestyle.

❏ **MEETINGS:** This is where you learn. Do you hate meetings? Get a tape player and listen to audio tapes. However, somewhere "down the line" you will have to attend meetings. Meetings can be fun. You will meet other people trying to do the same as you and you can learn from them. Meetings pump you up and can do the same for those you sponsor.

❏ **LISTEN:** Buy a good tape player with earphones, and use your CAR tape deck for listening and learning while you drive. ALL Network Marketing companies have scores of tapes. Get a telephone recording connector to plug your recorder into the phone line to record your company conference and training calls.

❏ **PHONE:** As you earn money, get better tools, like a quality telephone with a good answering machine. Get two telephone lines—and 3-way calling. Use the other as a dedicated fax line.

❏ **FAX:** A quality fax machine is essential for getting and sending messages quickly. This is no longer a luxury or a status symbol, it is a necessary *tool.*

❏ **HANDOUTS:** Always have business cards or company and product brochures to hand out, with your name, address and telephone number listed.

❏ **TAPES:** Buy as many audio tapes as you can afford, to hand out to those you prospect.

❏ **BOOKS:** Be smart and **USE THIS BOOK!** It's a *fantastic* marketing tool; the best I've ever seen.

❑ **COMPUTER:** As you grow, you'll want a computer for many reasons including access to your genealogy and volume. Most companies are automated with the latest telecommunications systems. If you think big and want to *be* big, you will eventually have to get the big tools. Computers save you money by allowing you e-mail correspondence—FREE!

Whether you are a newcomer or a veteran in Network Marketing, each company has their own *systems* that you must learn. To be successful you have to become a student again.

Part 1, The Student:

Because the human mind is so strong-willed and egotistical, one of the greatest challenges for any successful network marketer is to **break all of your old work habits that weren't successful.**

There are new ways that you must learn. You absolutely *must* become a student of these new ways and I plan to try them ALL!

The Network Marketing industry is growing so fast that it's often difficult to comprehend. There are 350,000 people EACH WEEK who are going into a home-based business.

The reasons are: layoffs, downsizing, hostile takeovers, bad management, competition, forced retirement, or just wanting to supplement income. Want to learn this business? Become a student.

Study your product line
Study your company
Study the industry of Network Marketing

It's not easy to be self-motivated, to work when it's more fun to play. But, it takes *money* to play. And, if you firmly believe in something and try to tell others about it, it's difficult to smile when you can see that they do *not* believe in what you fervently believe in.

One of the biggest reasons a person is **not** successful in Network Marketing is *their inability to handle rejection.* You can overcome this by study, by learning the answers, by learning to *counter* rejection. *Then*, rejection becomes a challenge, even fun.

Not *everyone* will listen to you; not *everyone* will buy what you have to sell; not *everyone* is bright enough to know a good opportunity when they see one. That's what I love about the book ideas Pete lists; you don't SELL, you only TELL. It truly works!

Another thing many new people in the business do is to spend hours and DAYS behind the computer trying to **reword** or **restructure** what is written and designed by *marketing experts.* Trust the fact, unless you're an advertising or marketing genius, the company literature is far better than what YOU can do. Just work *their* system!

Pete, with this book, went one step *beyond*! He didn't try to change or rewrite any *company* literature, he created an entire **new method** in Network Marketing. When I told him it was brilliant, he smiled and agreed.

I think one of the first qualifications for Network Marketing is if you LIKE PEOPLE because this is a *people* business. Hand out company brochures. Take what your sponsor has offered you as far as tools and systems and *go ballistic!* I did and it worked for me. It'll work for you too.

Part 2, The Mentor.

A MENTOR is an individual with a proven track record in the field in which you are planning to study. A mentor is someone you want to *mirror,* and by drawing from their wisdom and success you will make fewer mistakes.

The feeling I get is almost indescribable when I see someone that I trained and motivated become successful in Network Marketing. My heart swells with pride as I watch them grow and mature in their own home-based business and then go out and help and teach others to do the same.

Yes, I'm passionate about Network Marketing. It has changed my life so dramatically—and it can change yours. It happens to everyone who listens and learns in this business. We, in the industry, refer to it as your *learning curve,* the metamorphosis you go through from student to mentor. This can be a frightening transformation for some, going from a *sponge* for information and knowledge to the one who now teaches.

This puts you in a fish bowl; it means that you

are being watched, criticized, emulated, called upon to show others how to duplicate your habits—good and bad. It also means that your *organization* is growing, and as they look upon you for leadership, the responsibility is solely on your shoulders.

TIME MANAGEMENT has been mentioned a time or two in this book, and it is such an *important* work habit to teach as a good mentor. Whether you work your business part-time of full-time, you have only 24 hours to account for in each day.

If you manage your time *poorly*, it will consume you and offers little reward. A good mentor should be able to scan through their organization and spot the *rising* stars. Spend a large majority of your time with these people and both of your businesses will grow faster as a result. Here's why.

In Network Marketing (possibly any business) **20% of the people do 80% of the sales volume**. So, if you spend most of your time with that 20%, you are working to improve the majority of your sales and it will take less of your time! Makes sense, doesn't it? This is TIME MANAGEMENT.

Oftentimes, those of us who are passionate about this business and want to make millions, we might want success for our associate more than the associate wants success for themselves. That will never work; *you can't push a rope.* You must **sponsor** *for potential, but get **excited** over results.*

When a new, seemingly excellent person comes into your organization with all kinds of success stories, the first question you need to ask yourself is, *"Why aren't they still **with** that other company?"*

Perhaps the other company is no longer around. More often than not, they are the *jumpers,* the ones who vault from one company to the next looking for someone to *hand* them people and money. Don't waste your precious time on a talker, *jumper or malcontent,* just smile and move away.

I like to work with are the ones who ring my phone off the hook, those who are eager to learn what is going on in the company right now. This, more often than not, is a teachable student. If they show desire, spend your time wisely teaching *them*.

As a coach and mentor, it is your responsibility to show this new student the real BIG PICTURE of Network Marketing. Tell them that it takes study, and learning, and teaching, and *time*; it can't all happen in a month or several months. It might take a year, or two, or three.

Don't let me frighten you with this statement. I don't mean you'll starve during this time, quite the contrary. Just that the **BIG** money comes when you have a large organization and no matter how fast you are, it just takes time.

Oh, you'll still be living well if you work and teach, but to really get rich, it just takes T-I-M-E. Show me what other business you can get in and start at the very bottom, with absolutely no prior training, and earn $100,000 or more the first year!

A smart mentor must also try to get their new

associate a check **quickly**. If they don't reach a certain level of success in the first three months, either of three things usually happens.

① *You lose them forever.*
② *They quit and look for another Network Marketing company.*
③ *They will give Network Marketing a bad rap. It isn't entirely their fault, you have to accept part of the blame, also.*

That's why it's up to you, as mentor, to see that *realistic* goals are set, *systems* followed, and proper *work habits are* drilled in their heads. You must coach them every step of the way. It is up to you to teach them the *mechanics* of Network Marketing.

Stay *by their side* for their first 30 phone calls. Join *them* on their first 10 appointments. Conduct their first several interviews until your student learns to do it themselves.

By doing this, you will have an excited *student* on your hands. As they go through their *learning curve,* your business is growing as their's grows. If you are programming your time, you will have several students in training at the same time.

AUTHOR'S CLOSING COMMENTS

This really IS a fantastic CHANCE to make more money than you've ever dreamed possible, and it's true that just about anyone can do it. Donald Trump, in a recent television interview when asked what he'd do if he "lost it all," he answered **Network Marketing!**

Money is mentioned 98 times in this book because that's what the book is all about, how YOU can **earn lot's of money** and possibly get rich in Network Marketing.

Making money is like an *attitude.* Whether you think you *can* make money or you think you *can't*, you're right. Money has one sense—HEARING! If you tell it what to do, it'll work for you. Tell it *correctly* and it makes more. Tell it *incorrectly* and you make less.

I've been rich and I've been poor. Trust me, rich is better. I, personally, like the challenge; the *game.* Mostly I like to help others. When I vowed—way back when I was kid—not to be poor and to help those who needed help, I'm keeping that promise

I want to help YOU make a lot of money, meet wonderful new friends, enjoy what you're doing, and provide well for yourself and your loved ones. I want you to have FUN with your money, do good with it when you make it, and help others in any way you can. And You CAN through Network Marketing!

The

New
Millionaires

is available through:

Swan Publishing
126 Live Oak
Alvin, TX 77511

(281) 388-2547
Fax (281) 585-3738

or e-mail: swanbooks@ghg.net

Visit our web site at:
http:\\www.swan-pub.com

Afer reading this book, please pass it on to a friend or relative. It could change their lives for the better—FOREVER.

ABOUT THE AUTHOR

PETE BILLAC is one of the most sought-after speakers in the United States. He has written 47 full-length books, hundreds of short stories and he makes his audiences laugh—hard. His worldwide best seller, HOW NOT TO BE LONELY, sold over four million copies.

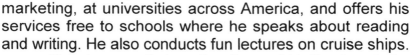

Pete is a maverick; he writes what pleases him. His topics range from adventure, war, the Mafia, and famous people, to romance, love, health and motivation.

He gives seminars for Fortune 500 companies on marketing, at universities across America, and offers his services free to schools where he speaks about reading and writing. He also conducts fun lectures on cruise ships.

Pete is currently traveling the world telling how to be successful with Network Marketing and on his newest book, *Managing Stress*. "*This book tells people how to become rich. Making money is great—and easy, too, if you believe in yourself and work smart. God wants you to be prosperous, and to help others along the way.*"

Perhaps you've seen Pete on Donahue, Sally Jessy Raphael, Good Morning America, Laff Stop and other national televison shows. He mixes common sense and knowledge with laughter. He charms his audiences, and breathes life into every topic.

"Pete is an expert at restoring self-confidence and self-esteem in others . . ."
Phil Donahue
National Television Talk Show Host